My First **NFL** Book

DETROIT
LIONS

Steven M. Karras

www.av2books.com

LET'S READ
AV²
BY WEIGL™
ADDED VALUE • AUDIO VISUAL

Go to **www.av2books.com**, and enter this book's unique code.

BOOK CODE

R 282444

AV² by Weigl brings you media enhanced books that support active learning.

AV² provides enriched content that supplements and complements this book. Weigl's AV² books strive to create inspired learning and engage young minds in a total learning experience.

Your AV² Media Enhanced books come alive with...

Audio
Listen to sections of the book read aloud.

Key Words
Study vocabulary, and complete a matching word activity.

Video
Watch informative video clips.

Quizzes
Test your knowledge.

Embedded Weblinks
Gain additional information for research.

Slide Show
View images and captions, and prepare a presentation.

Try This!
Complete activities and hands-on experiments.

... and much, much more!

Published by AV² by Weigl
350 5th Avenue, 59th Floor
New York, NY 10118

Website: www.av2books.com

Printed in the United States of America in Brainerd, Minnesota
1 2 3 4 5 6 7 8 9 0 21 20 19 18 17

032017
020317

Editor: Katie Gillespie
Art Director: Terry Paulhus

Weigl acknowledges Getty Images and iStock as the primary image suppliers for this title.

Library of Congress Control Number: 2017930539

ISBN 978-1-4896-5505-9 (hardcover)
ISBN 978-1-4896-5507-3 (multi-user eBook)

DETROIT LIONS

CONTENTS

Team History

The Detroit Lions joined the NFL in 1930. They were first called the Portsmouth Spartans and played in Ohio. The team moved to Detroit, Michigan, in 1934. The Lions won their first NFL championship in their second year.

Billy Sims was the Lions' first overall draft pick in 1980.

The Stadium

The Lions play their home games at Ford Field. It is an indoor stadium. The stadium was built in 2002. It was designed so fans can see the field clearly from different seats. Ford Field is the Lions' sixth stadium.

Ford Field has a glass wall on one end so visitors can see the skyline of Detroit, Michigan.

Team Spirit

The Lions' mascot is Roary. Roary greets fans as they enter the stadium on game days. He also takes pictures with Lions fans. Roary is in charge of the Cub Club. This is a Lions fan club for kids. Roary's favorite song is the Lions' fight song, "Gridiron Heroes."

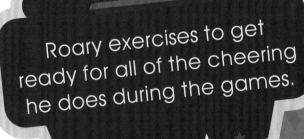

Roary exercises to get ready for all of the cheering he does during the games.

The Jerseys

The Lions' colors are silver, blue, and white. Players wear blue jerseys with silver pants for home games. They wear white jerseys and silver pants for away games. The front of the jersey has a patch with the letters "WCF." This stands for William Clay Ford, Sr. He was a former owner of the team.

The Helmet

The Lions' helmets are silver. Blue, white, and black stripes go down the middle of the helmet. The team logo is on each side. The logo was changed in 2009 to make the lion larger. Eyes, fangs, and more fur were also added to the lion.

The first NFL helmets were made out of leather.

The Coach

Jim Caldwell has been the head coach of the Lions since 2014. Caldwell is the first African American head coach for the team. The Lions won 11 games during his first year. This set a record for the most wins by a Lions head coach in his first season.

Player Positions

The defense tries to stop the other team's offense from scoring. Players called linebackers stop the other team from running with the ball or catching passes. There are also players called tackles. They stop the quarterback from passing the ball.

Cornerbacks also try to stop receivers from catching passes.

Matthew Stafford is a quarterback. He was the Lions' first draft pick in 2009. Stafford is one of only six NFL quarterbacks in history to throw 4,000 or more yards in four straight seasons. He set the NFL record for most completed passing yards in his first 50 games. Stafford has thrown 187 touchdown passes.

Barry Sanders was the Lions' running back from 1989 to 1998. He rushed 100 or more yards per game in 14 games during the 1997 season. This is an NFL record. Sanders was invited to the Pro Bowl each year of his career. The best NFL players from different teams are chosen to play in the Pro Bowl every year.

Famous Player

19

Team Records

The Lions have won four NFL championships. Linebacker Chris Spielman holds the team record for 195 tackles in one season. Former wide receiver Calvin Johnson holds many team records. He made 731 catches and scored 83 receiving touchdowns. He also set NFL records for most receiving yards and most receiving touchdowns.

4 NFL Championships

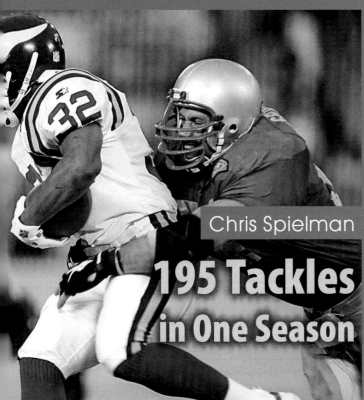

Chris Spielman

195 Tackles in One Season

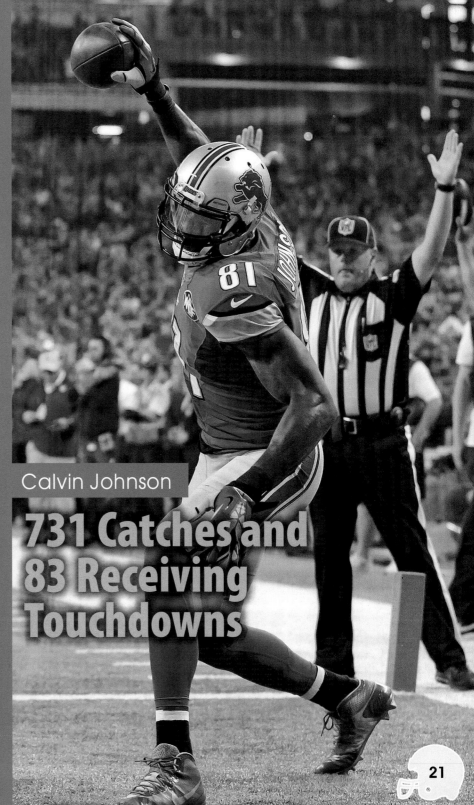

Calvin Johnson

731 Catches and 83 Receiving Touchdowns

By the Numbers

Wide receiver Herman Moore holds the team record for **14** catches in a single game.

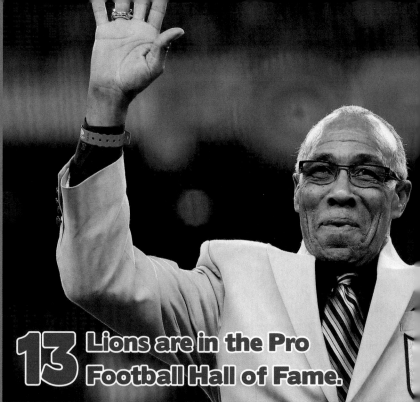

13 Lions are in the Pro Football Hall of Fame.

Ford Field can seat up to **65,000 people**.

The Lions only allowed the Chicago Cardinals to move **14** total yards during a game in 1940.

Kicker Jason Hanson holds a team record for scoring **495** field goals in his career.

5

Lions player numbers have been retired.

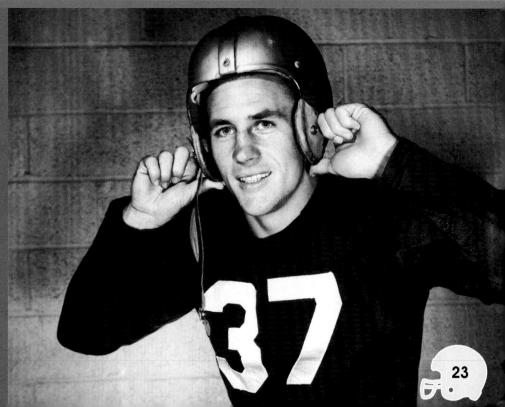

Quiz

1. When did the Lions win their first NFL championship?

2. What is Roary's favorite song?

3. What does "WCF" stand for?

4. Which Lions player scored 83 receiving touchdowns?

5. How many field goals did Jason Hanson score?

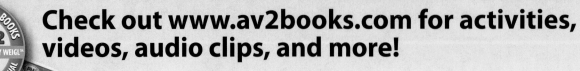
www.av2books.com